THE
BERMUDA
TRIANGLE
BY
HARRIETTE ABELS

EDITED BY
Dr. Howard Schroeder
Professor in Reading and Language Arts
Dept. of Curriculum and Instruction
Mankato State University

PUBLISHED BY

CRESTWOOD HOUSE

CIP

LIBRARY OF CONGRESS CATALOGING IN PUBLICATION DATA

Abels, Harriette Sheffer.
Bermuda Triangle.

(The Mystery of ——)
SUMMARY: Recounts some of the mysterious disappearances of ships and planes in that area of the Atlantic Ocean called the Bermuda Triangle.
1. Bermuda Triangle—Juvenile literature. 2. Bermuda Triangle. I. Schroeder, Howard.   I. Title.
G558.A24   1987   001.9'4   87-14029
ISBN 0-89686-340-9

International Standard Book Number: 0-89686-340-9	Library of Congress Catalog Card Number: 87-14029

CREDITS

Illustrations:
Cover Illustration: Bob Williams
National Aeronautics and Space Administration (NASA): 5
UPI/Bettmann Newsphotos: 6, 8-9
Bob Williams: 11, 13, 14, 18-19, 20-21, 24-25, 27, 29, 31, 33, 39, 45
AP/Wide World Photos: 22-23, 36-37
The Bettmann Archive, Inc.: 35
Fortean Picture Library: 40
Pino G. Turolla: 42-43
Andy Schlabach: 46
Graphic Design & Production:
Baker Street Productions, Ltd.

CRESTWOOD·HOUSE

Box 3427, Mankato, MN, U.S.A. 56002

THE BERMUDA TRIANGLE

TABLE OF CONTENTS

Chapter 1

It doesn't look any different from other parts of the ocean. The waters are blue and deep. Waves lap at the sandy shores of beaches, and seagulls fly through the air. But something is wrong. At least once a year, a plane or a ship disappears in this area, never to be heard from again.

This mysterious place is sometimes called the Devil's Triangle . . . or the Sea of Lost Souls . . . or the Atlantic's Graveyard. It is also called the Bermuda Triangle.

It is easy to find the Bermuda Triangle on a map. It runs from the Bermuda Islands, south to Puerto Rico, and west to Miami, Florida. The area covers about forty-four thousand square miles (113,960 sq. km).

Since 1945, over one hundred planes and ships—and more than a thousand people—have been lost in this strange area. There are rarely any signs of wreckage or bodies found after a disappearance. Ship and plane wrecks happen all over the world, but there is usually something to mark the site. There may be debris from a smashed plane, or an oil slick. Other times there may be the remains of a ship's hull, or drifting lifeboats.

This photo was taken from outer space and shows the area off the tip of Florida called the "Bermuda Triangle."

Avenger torpedo bombers like these were used by Flight 19 in 1945.

But in the Bermuda Triangle, there is nothing! It's as if the ocean has swallowed everything.

Not every ship or plane that passes through the Triangle disappears. In fact, it is a well-traveled area. Planes and ships move through the waters and air every day without seeing anything unusual. And yet, strange events keep happening. At least once a year there is a disappearance somewhere within the Triangle.

The most famous disappearance happened on December 5, 1945. On this day, six navy planes and their crews disappeared forever. It was this incident that gave the Triangle its name.

The first five planes of Flight 19 were on a training mission from the naval air station at Fort Lauderdale, Florida. The flight plan stretched from Fort Lauderdale, 160 miles (257 km) east, then 40 miles (64 km) to the north, before returning to the base. The tip of the triangle formed by the flight plan was in a direct line with Bermuda.

The commander of Flight 19 was Lieutenant Charles Taylor. All of the pilots and crew members were experienced flyers. They went first to Chicken Shoals, north of Bimini, where they practiced bombing runs on an old ship hull. At about 3:15 p.m., the five-plane group headed east. Suddenly, the radio man at the naval air tower in Fort Lauderdale received a strange message from Lieutenant Taylor.

"Calling tower. This is an emergency . . . we seem to be off course . . . we cannot see land. Repeat . . . we cannot see land . . . we are not sure of our position . . . we seem to be lost."

7

The controller told them that their bearing was due west. But Lieutenant Taylor said that they didn't know which was west. Everything looked different than it should have. Strange messages came in over the next few minutes. "Both of my compasses are out. I am trying to find Fort Lauderdale . . . I'm sure I am in the Keys, but I don't know how far down."

The messages became harder to hear because of static. It seemed that the flight could no longer hear the replies from the tower. But the tower could hear conversations among the five crews. Some of the pilots

While searching for Flight 19, a Martin Mariner "Flying Boat" like this one was also lost at sea.

talked about running out of fuel. Others said that the gyroscopes and magnetic compasses in all the planes were off and were "going crazy." They all showed a different reading.

While this was going on, the controller at Fort Lauderdale wasn't able to make any contact with the planes. By now, the workers at the naval base were aware that something was very wrong with Flight 19. Rescue craft were sent out, including a Martin Mariner "Flying Boat" plane that held a crew of thirteen men.

At 4:00 p.m. the tower heard a message saying that

Lieutenant Taylor had turned over his command to a pilot named Captain Stiver. Captain Stiver's message was even more puzzling. "We must have passed over Florida and are now in the Gulf of Mexico," the workers heard him say. Stiver must have decided to turn back, hoping this would return them to Florida. But as the flight made the turn, their radio signal began to fade. The tower workers knew that the aircraft had made a wrong turn and were flying east, away from Florida.

The Martin Mariner was sent on its way to the general area where it was thought Flight 19 had gotten lost. Its crew radioed back that there were strong winds at altitudes above six thousand feet (1,829 m). But then the messages stopped.

Soon it became obvious that this plane had also disappeared. No one ever heard from Flight 19 or the Martin Mariner rescue plane again.

Coast Guard vessels continued to look for survivors during the night, but found nothing. The next day, at daybreak, an official search was started. It was one of the largest searches in U.S. naval history, involving more than three hundred planes, many ships and even a few submarines. Hundreds of private citizens joined the search in their planes, yachts and boats. But nothing was ever found—not an oil slick, not a piece of debris, not one body washed ashore. For weeks, the beaches along the coast of Florida and the Bahamas were checked daily for wreckage. Nothing ever appeared.

There are many unanswered questions about the missing Flight 19. Why were no SOS messages received, either from Flight 19 or the Martin Mariner? The Avenger planes of Flight 19 were able to make smooth, easy water landings. Their crews were trained to abandon ship in sixty seconds. Life rafts were available. What affected the compasses and gyroscopes? And why did Lieutenant Taylor turn over the command of the flight to another officer? The disappearance of Flight 19 is one of the greatest mysteries in the history of the U.S. naval forces.

The disappearance of Flight 19 and the Martin Mariner is one of the biggest mysteries of the U.S. Navy.

Chapter 2

There are many pages of reports of lost craft in the Bermuda Triangle.

The *Carroll A. Deering* was a large schooner. One stormy morning in January of 1929, it sailed into the Diamond Shoals at the Cape Hatteras Coast Guard station in North Carolina. The ship had its sails up. The rescue team that set out for the ship couldn't believe that the schooner would be in full sail on such a stormy day. If the sails had been trimmed or lowered, it would never have landed on the shoals.

Because of the weather, it took four days for the rescue team to get to the ship. When they did, they couldn't believe their eyes. Not one person was on board. On the stove was a meal of soup, meat and vegetables. It seemed that the ship had been abandoned shortly before a dinner meal. But there didn't seem to be a reason for the crew to have left the ship. There was nothing wrong with the vessel.

The rescuers now realized why the schooner had been in full sail—the captain and crew must have left during calm weather. That made no sense at all. Why would the crew leave the ship if they were not in danger? It was wintertime, and the waters were icy cold. Surely

In 1929, the Carroll A. Deering sailed into the Diamond Shoals off the coast of North Carolina. Although it was a stormy day, the ship was in full sail.

13

Not one person was aboard the vessel.

experienced sailors would know that they would have little chance of staying alive in small lifeboats. As long as the ship was afloat, they would be much safer staying on board.

It seemed as if the crew had left in a very orderly fashion. The ship's papers, records, and chronometer were missing. Also gone were some of the crew's extra clothing. The captain's personal belongings were also gone, along with a large trunk. It wouldn't have been possible to put such a heavy object into a small lifeboat.

One of the charts still on the ship showed that the captain had been in command until a week before the schooner was found. At that point the handwriting changed. No one knows whether the captain died or became ill. Perhaps he was washed overboard in a storm.

During the investigation, it was discovered that the captain had been having some problems with the crew. Maybe the ship had been boarded by pirates. Two days before the ship was found, it had sailed by a lightship called *The Cape Lookout.* The captain of *The Cape Lookout* later said that he had thought at the time that something was wrong. The sailors aboard seemed to be standing around doing very little. Their captain was nowhere in sight. A man with red hair and a foreign accent called to the lightship over a megaphone. He reported that the *Deering* had lost its anchors in a storm and asked the lightship captain to report the loss.

The captain of *The Cape Lookout* didn't know what

to think. Usually the captain of a ship passed on such messages. Also, the red-haired man had not identified himself. He didn't look like a ship's officer. The captain of the lightship was confused. If *Deering's* captain was sick or dead, why hadn't it been reported? That fact was a lot more important than the loss of the anchors.

The investigators were puzzled when the captain of the lightship made his report. No man answering to the description of the red-haired man had been aboard when the ship sailed from Barbados. How had he gotten there?

They were never able to move the *Carroll A. Deering* from the shoals where she had run aground. A few months later, a storm tossed her about until she broke up. No member of her crew was ever heard from again. Unless the entire crew was killed and thrown overboard by pirates, they too had disappeared into the Devil's Triangle.

Chapter 3

Seafarers have known about the Triangle for centuries. But it wasn't until World War II that people realized that airplanes—flying over the same area—could also vanish from the sky.

In January, 1948, a four-motor passenger plane disappeared while flying from the Azores to Bermuda. When the plane was 380 miles (611 km) northeast of Bermuda, the pilot radioed that the weather was excellent and they would arrive on schedule. But the plane never arrived, nor was an SOS received. By the following day, a thorough search operation was underway. Some boxes and empty oil drums were found northwest of Bermuda two days later. But if they belonged to that plane, it would mean that it had flown hundreds of miles off course. That seems impossible, since the pilot's last message said nothing about being lost.

One year later, a similar plane, carrying thirteen passengers and a crew of seven, disappeared between Bermuda and Jamaica. When this second plane took off from Bermuda, the sea was calm and the weather was good. A normal flight report was made by the captain an hour later.

"We have reached cruising altitude. Fair weather.

Expected time of arrival in Kingston as scheduled. I am changing radio frequency to pick up Kingston.''

But the captain never contacted the Kingston, Jamaica tower. That message to Bermuda was the last anyone ever heard of the plane.

Another passenger plane, a chartered DC-3 going from San Juan to Miami, had disappeared in the same area two weeks earlier. The facts of this flight's disappearance could not be explained. The weather was excellent and the night was clear. The plane took off from San Juan at 10:30 p.m. At 4:13 a.m., the Miami

In 1949, the pilot of a DC-3 reported seeing the lights of Miami— but the plane never landed.

tower received this message: "We are approaching the field . . . only fifty miles to the south . . . we can see the lights of Miami now. All's well. Will stand by for landing instructions."

The plane never landed. A land-and-sea search found no wreckage. If the plane was truly only fifty miles (80 km) south of Miami, why was there no SOS or no flares? The plane simply vanished over the Florida Keys. The waters there are shallow and clear. How could a plane with thirty-six passengers and crew members, almost within sight of the landing field, vanish so completely?

Four technicians watch in amazement as an Air Force jet disappears from their radar screens.

Many of the strange disappearances have been on flights from the Florida Homestead Air Force Base. In September, 1971, a captain and lieutenant flew a jet fighter over the Atlantic. At the base, four technicians tracked its flight on radar. Suddenly the jet simply disappeared from the radar screen! It happened so fast that it took the technicians a few minutes to realize what had happened. Immediately, search planes were sent

out to find the missing plane. It should have been a simple search-and-rescue operation. The technicians knew exactly where the plane was when it dropped from the radar screen. The time was early morning and visibility was excellent. In the area where the plane had disappeared, the water was shallow and clear. But, once again, no trace of the missing plane was ever found.

In October, 1971, a plane disappeared right before the eyes of a group of scientists. This happened a short distance away from an ocean research vessel called *The Discoverer*. A four-engine plane seemed to come to a complete stop in midair, then plunged straight down into the ocean. The ship reached the site of the crash in a few minutes. There was nothing left. The scientists aboard, who had seen the plane drop, were amazed.

Scientists aboard **The Discoverer** *witnessed a plane drop from the sky—then vanish!*

A sharp dive like that should have smashed the plane to pieces. But there was no wreckage at all.

The Discoverer had modern sonar equipment on board. But the graphs showed no sign of the plane. The scientists knew they had seen the plane fall. They also knew there was no trace of the plane either on the surface or under the water. They couldn't offer any explanation.

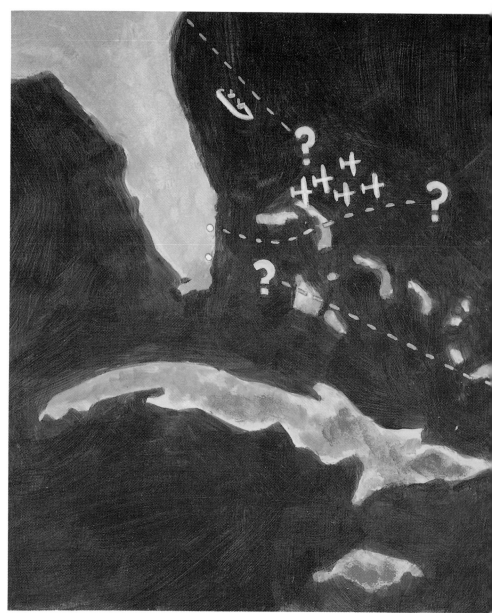

This illustration shows the paths of some of the ships and planes
that later were lost in the Devil's Triangle. No definite pattern has
been established.

25

Chapter 4

Many of the aircraft lost in the Bermuda Triangle were commercial flights or owned by the military. These disappearances were well documented. But many smaller planes have also vanished.

In August, 1963, two four-engine planes went down three hundred miles (483 km) southwest of Bermuda. At first, it was thought that this was another total disappearance. Some wreckage, however, was found 260 miles (418 km) southwest of Bermuda. Some people thought that the two planes had somehow crashed into each other. But more debris surfaced several days later, 160 miles (257 km) away. That seemed strange. If the planes had collided in the air, something must have separated the wreckage much more quickly than the natural ocean currents could have done. Also, Air Force officials said the planes were not flying close enough together to have collided. If that is true, what caused their engines or instruments to go out at the same time?

In June, 1965, a small plane carrying a crew of ten vanished on a flight from Florida to Grand Turk Island near the Bahamas. Its last report gave their position as one hundred miles (161 km) from Grand Turk. They also gave an estimated time of arrival (E.T.A.) of one

When two planes went down southwest of Bermuda in 1963, people feared they had collided. The wreckage from the two planes, however, was found 160 miles (257 km) apart.

27

hour. When they didn't arrive, a search was started that lasted five days and nights.

In this case, as with some of the other vanished planes, faint messages that could not be understood were picked up and then faded out. They sounded as if the plane was moving farther and farther into space.

In 1967, the cruise ship, *Queen Elizabeth I,* was moving through the Triangle. Two sailors on deck saw a small plane flying about three hundred yards (274 m) away. Suddenly, the plane started flying straight toward the ship. The sailors froze, certain that it would crash into the *Queen.* But one hundred yards (91 m) away, the plane disappeared. There was no sound, no splash, no air bubbles. The plane simply vanished. The sailors reported the incident to the captain, but no one believed them.

Another case involved a woman pilot and a passenger in a small plane. They were flying from Nassau in the Bahamas to Grand Turk Island. When the pilot reached the area where she thought Grand Turk should be, she radioed that she was unable to find her direction. She said she was circling over two unidentified islands.

"Nothing is down there," she said. A short time later, she asked "Is there any way out of this?" The plane disappeared and was never seen again. But observers on the island had seen a small plane circling the island for about half an hour before it disappeared. If they could see the plane, why was the pilot unable to see the buildings on Grand Turk Island?

People on Grand Turk Island watched as a small plane circled above them. After half an hour, the plane flew off—and was never heard or seen again.

29

Chapter 5

There is one famous survivor of an unexplained experience in the Devil's Triangle. In fact, this man survived it twice.

Dick Stern lives in Atlanta, Georgia. He was in the Air Corps during World War II. His first experience in the Triangle happened in December of 1944. Seven bombers left the United States for Italy. On the way, they stopped in Bermuda to refuel and to rest.

They left the island at night for the flight across the Atlantic. There was a full moon and the air was clear. They were an hour out of Bermuda when suddenly everything went wrong. The plane Stern was in flipped over on its back, going completely out of control. Only the pilot and co-pilot had seat belts. The other nine men were tossed around like sacks of flour. One moment they were on the ceiling and the next they were on the floor. The pilot and co-pilot were experienced flyers and strong men besides. They fought hard to regain altitude, but the strange force that held them wouldn't let go. Somehow, at the last possible moment when the plane was almost in the water, they were able to pull the plane free of the strange force. No one on the plane was in any condition to continue on to Italy. The pilot

In 1944, seven bombers from the U.S. Army Air Corps went out of control an hour out of Bermuda. Only two of the planes made it back.

turned back to Bermuda.

As soon as they landed, they were told that five of the other six bombers that had left the island with them had been lost at sea. There had been no distress call from any of them. They were just gone! All of this happened in a little more than an hour. The search turned up no sign of the planes. The pilots of the two planes that made it back had no explanation for what had happened to them.

The missing planes, too, must have flown into a strange force. But what? Could it have simply been air turbulence? Airplanes encounter rough air all the time. But no pilot has ever described anything like the two pilots did on this occasion.

The Air Corps authorities were puzzled. They had no idea what had happened. The weather was clear. Seven pilots could not possibly make the same mistake at the same time. The planes were in good working order. No one could figure out what had caused seven big bombers to go out of control.

Seventeen years later, Dick Stern and his wife were on a flight from London, England, to Miami, Florida. They were on a commercial plane scheduled to stop at Bermuda and Nassau. Just as lunch was served, the plane suddenly dropped straight down. The plane was tossed back and forth, up and down, while food, drinks, papers and other objects were tossed wildly about. The crew tried to bring the plane under control, but they were totally helpless. There were no dark clouds nor any evidence of air turbulence. The fight for control of the aircraft went on for over fifteen minutes. Then suddenly it ended, as quickly as it had begun. The rest of the trip to the Bahamas was smooth.

Dick Stern experienced the Bermuda Triangle again in 1961 while flying from England to Miami. The commercial airliner flew out of control for fifteen minutes.

33

Chapter 6

Many explanations have been given for the mysteries of the Bermuda Triangle. Many books and articles have been written about it. The authors all seem to have their own ideas about what is going on.

In 1918, the *U.S.S. Cyclops* took on a load of coal at Norfolk, Virginia, to be moved to U.S. warships off the coast of Brazil. They made it to Rio de Janeiro and began the return trip with a load of manganese ore. Two weeks later, the Navy realized that the ship was missing. The writer of a newspaper article thought that the *Cyclops* might have been sunk by a giant octopus, which dragged it to the bottom of the sea. But the *Cyclops* weighed nineteen thousand tons (17,233 MT) and was almost six hundred feet (183 m) long! No octopus could be that strong!

For years, waterspouts and other odd water conditions were blamed for the missing ships. But once it was realized that airplanes were also disappearing, that theory had to be thrown out. An airplane may have mechanical trouble, but the waves twenty thousand feet (6,096 m) below would have no effect on it.

Mel Fisher, a famous undersea treasure hunter, thinks that some of the disappearances may have been caused

One newspaper reporter suggested that the U.S.S. Cyclops was destroyed by a giant octopus!

The 1918 disappearance of the U.S.S. Cyclops *is still a mystery today.*

by unexploded bombs. He thinks there may be old, live torpedoes left from past wars. There may even be live bombs from combat training exercises that take place today.

Fisher also says that there is a great deal of quicksand where the gulf stream flows past the end of Florida. It is known that these quicksands can "swallow" fairly large boats which get stuck in the sandy bottom.

Officials of the United States Coast Guard say there is nothing unusual or mysterious about the events in the Triangle. Their explanation is that the amount of air and sea traffic in the Triangle is very heavy. When a ship disappears, it can be blamed on strange environmental events. They say that the gulf stream is choppy and swift. The weather in the Caribbean-Atlantic area changes rapidly. Thunderstorms and waterspouts appear without warning. Also, the ocean floor in the Bermuda area has some of the deepest trenches in the world. This may explain why the debris from wrecks is seldom found.

In 1969, Bill Verity sailed from Ireland to Fort Lauderdale, Florida, in a twenty-foot boat made out of plywood. The trip took him 115 days. He said that the worst part of the trip was a lightning storm that took place when he was sailing through the Bermuda Triangle. Verity said, "Never have I seen such lightning—bolt after bolt struck the water." He said the storm kept up that night and all the next day. He was terrified.

Also in 1969, an Englishman named John Fairfax was the first man to row a boat across the Atlantic all alone. It took him six months to go from the Canary Islands to Fort Lauderdale. When he arrived, he told a strange tale of an event that happened in the Triangle. He said there were two "flying saucers" that tried to cut short his voyage. They looked like two bright lights. He was sure they were not stars. The two objects went higher into the sky and then separated, one flying low and the other high. Then they were gone. Fairfax said that while the two objects were visible, he had a strange feeling. He had the feeling that someone was telling him to go away.

A charter boat captain named John Carpenter heard John Fairfax tell his story. Carpenter thought that Fairfax was just trying to get attention. But a year later, he changed his mind.

In 1969, Bill Verity encountered a terrifying storm in the Bermuda Triangle.

Waterspouts occur rapidly and can sink a ship. This artist's view of waterspouts was created in Paris in 1888.

Carpenter was returning from Bimini on his charter boat. Shortly after midnight, he stared out over the ocean, trying to see the lights of Fort Lauderdale. He began to feel that something odd was happening. It took him a few minutes to realize what was wrong. Then he saw that the light shining on the deck was not the white light of the moon's glow. Instead, the light was green. He leaned out of the cabin window. Directly above the boat were two glowing, disc-shaped objects. They just hovered there. Carpenter was about to call the other people onto the deck when the two objects dropped into the sea almost without a splash. The glow from the objects continued until they were deep into the water.

A psychic in Miami has very strong feelings about the Triangle. He thinks that half of the disappearances come from natural causes. Of the remaining mysteries, some are supernatural only in the sense that whatever causes them is something with which our scientists are not familiar. But this psychic has also had very strong visions about the scientific reason for the disappearances.

He thinks that the pilots suffocate because the air is pulled from their lungs. They can't breath. Even the oxygen and pressurized cabins can't give them enough air. He described the happening as a huge whirlpool that comes from a hole in the floor of the ocean. When this whirlpool reaches the surface of the water, it pulls in all of the air around it. It can pull down ships—and

Some people feel that the lost continent of Atlantis is located in the Bermuda Triangle. In this picture, a diver examines stone formations found off the coast of Bimini.

anything else that floats—without leaving a trace. He says it can also pull in airplanes flying as high as ten thousand feet (3,048 m).

"When I have this vision," he says, "the breath is sucked from my lungs. I have trouble breathing."

The Bermuda Triangle covers an area of the Atlantic where some people think the lost continent of Atlantis supposedly sank. Edgar Cayce, an American psychic, said that the ancient Atlanteans used crystals as a power source. Many of the stories about disappearances in the Bermuda Triangle talk about a strange magnetic pull on the compasses and electronic equipment used in today's ships and planes. Is it possible that an Atlantean crystal power source, lying beneath the ocean for more than ten thousand years, is responsible for today's tragedies?

The Bermuda Triangle is not the only place in the world where a strange magnetic force seems to be at work. There are nine other areas, all in the shape of a triangle and all located near the equator. The magnetic forces are easy to find. They do strange things to electrical equipment. No one knows the source of this strange power.

People who believe in UFO's feel that the Triangle is some kind of "collecting station" for aliens from outer space. In this theory, spaceships come from other planets. They cause problems with the magnetic fields. Then they take the planes, ships and people onto their spaceships, back to their own planets.

The Bermuda Triangle is still a mystery.

Another theory is that there is an advanced civilization under the ocean. Perhaps these beings grab the ships and planes and pull them down. Other people think that the vessels have disappeared into "another dimension." That is, the planes and ships still exist, but in such a way that we can no longer see them.

There have been many investigations into the strange happenings in the Bermuda Triangle. Many investigations . . . but no real answers.

45

Map

The Bermuda
Triangle covers the
area between
Miami (Florida),
Puerto Rico, and
Bermuda.

Glossary/Index

47